My Five Stages of Grief

A Father's Journey to Recovery from Bereavement

By Darren Heart

Print Edition
ISBN: 978-1499136210

http://www.darrenheart.com

Copyright, Legal Notice and Disclaimer

Foreword

My Five Stages of Grief by Darren Heart is an emotional chronicle of the author's ten year journey of recovery and healing from the grief and overwhelming sense of loss caused by the tragic deaths of his long term partner, and shortly afterwards, his step son.

The Prologue for this book summarizes the author's moving love story up until the moment tragedy strikes at the heart of his family. The main body is represented by five chapters dedicated to the five stages of grief, namely; Denial, Anger, Bargaining, Depression and Acceptance. Each chapter is broken down to include a brief clinical definition for a particular stage, followed by the author's own observations and experiences, closing with a number of poems written by the author, intended to reflect upon the various emotions and thoughts he experienced during that particular stage of the grieving process. Concluding with an Epilogue where the author describes life "post-acceptance" and offers words of hope, inspiration and encouragement to those who may be wading through the grief and mourning process and feeling misunderstood or isolated.

Contains original emotional, and thought provoking poems, capturing the author's raw thoughts and emotions associated with each stage. For those who have suffered the loss of a loved one, this book explores a mourner's need to acknowledge death and embrace the pain of loss and bereavement as a pathway to recovery.

At one time or another, we will all find ourselves facing a dark journey through the grieving process. My Five Stages of Grief is written to provide support and comfort for a person who is in the wake of despair following the loss of a loved one.

Table of Contents

Prologue

When deciding exactly where to start my story it became obvious to me immediately that my story starts the day I met the love of my life, Claire. Sat on a park style bench at the top of a green hill overlooking Portsmouth Harbor, watching her two young children play in front of her, Claire sat patiently, waiting for the arrival of what could only be described as her blind date. This was the day that we met.

It was the spring of 1996 and I had been living alone with my daughter Victoria for several years following the departure of her mother to Ireland to pursue a new life with her new boyfriend. Since our divorce some years earlier I had struggled to be satisfied that my daughter was being properly cared for and had been fighting a long battle for custody. No tears were shed the day I received a phone call from Victoria's mother at around 3pm asking if we can talk. By 5pm that day Victoria was in my care and her mother had left for a new life in Ireland.

The new role of a lone parent took some time to adjust to, having an effect on so many aspects of ones life. While most of my friends were going out on a regular basis, even those with partners as none of my friends had children yet, I would need to arrange childcare and so my social life dwindled into the realms of school runs and shopping trips.

I had previously run my own computer sales and repair business and so computers, and the fact I am a nerd, gave me plenty to do with my time. One particular fascination was the pre-internet concept of dial-up services. The idea that simply connecting a small box to my computer and phone line, and enduring a blast of screeches and bleeps, would allow my computer to communicate with lots of others computers, blew my mind, nerd heaven!

So there I was, navigating news databases and other useless information, while feeling like a character from a sci-fi movie such as *War Games*, when I stumbled across the term "Forum". I think my attention was drawn to this word because up until now my experience with dial-up services had been very sterile. Information stored and transferred on computers seemed a long away removed from the public nature of what I knew to be a forum, so I selected the appropriate menu option and took a peak.

I sat staring at what seemed to be a largely empty screen, wondering if there had been some kind of transfer error, when a line of text appeared at the top of the screen, shortly followed by another, and then another. I had walked into what today would be described as an internet chat room. After some time consisting of just reading the conversation, I took the plunge and sent my first message, to be welcomed by a host of messages saying hello, and making me feel most welcome. Now this was cool!

"Delilah" impressed me from the moment she started speaking in the chat room. It was hard to resist the pull of her humor and after a short time became my partner in crime. I had previously discovered a way to send audio clips into the chat room, much to the moderator's annoyance, and we spent many evenings running our own little radio station within the chat room, with Delilah selecting and sourcing the audio clips, while broadcasting them myself.

The first time we spoke on the telephone was one of those never to be forgotten, life changing moments, or should I say fourteen hours straight of moments! I had never dreamed it possible that two people could talk for such a long time without ever feeling stuck for something to say, or boredom setting in. More surprising, after such a marathon phone call, we were both eager to talk again, after sleeping of course!

This brings us back to the occasion on the hill. Several weeks had passed since we started building enormous phone bills, and the decision to actually meet had been made. I remember sitting in the car park, starring at her back, battling with the usual questions; What if she doesn't like me? Will we get on? What will I say? Oh, the irony of that one!

After taking a deep breath and summoning my best "Right, let's do this!" inner voice, I exit the car and went to meet my fate. It was a beautiful day, and as I approached the sun seemed to focus solely on her, more so as she looked up at me, stood before her, smiling in the sunlight. No words were spoken, we simply kissed, and... I think we kissed some more. What will I say? Well I think my first attempts at words may have been wow, or something along those lines. And so began our love story...

I think love can be measured in a number of ways, intensity and scope among them. For this reason I would describe Claire (a.k.a. Delilah), without hesitation, as the love of my life. Intensity was not an issue, our relationship had energy of its own, but the scope of our love was as diverse as it was intense. She was caring and motherly, needy like a little sister, loving like a partner, and much like that mischievous best friend you get into trouble with, you know the one!

Within six months of our initial speechless hill top encounter, Claire had moved in with me, my daughter Victoria, along with her two younger children, Emily and Oliver, also joined by my son Daniel most weekends, making up my new, but yet to be completed, family.

Close to four years later saw the arrival of our beautiful daughter Millennia, completing our family portrait. These were, without doubt, the best days of my life.

It's hard to describe in simple terms the many intricacies of human relationships, but I always saw my relationship with Claire as a well oiled machine, with all the cogs in all the right places, some cogs were hers and others were my own. Partners in all respects, facing everything life had to throw at us together as a team. So powerful was the output of this machine that I finally came to truly understand the phrase *more than the sum of its parts*.

The autumn of 2002 brought with it a fall in fortune along with the falling leaves. Claire, now working as a manager for an insurance company, and keen to make a good impression in this new role, decided to attend the local hospital with concerns regarding what she believed to be a chest infection. Believing that starting a course of antibiotics sooner rather than later would be of benefit, and reduce the likelihood that she would need to take any time off work so soon after her promotion, it was decided not to wait until after the weekend when our family doctors surgery would be open.

After dropping Claire at the hospital I returned home to look after our children, and working from home most days anyway, continue my own work. After a number of hours passed Claire called to ask if I could take her some night cloths and other assorted items as the hospital had requested she stay in overnight for more tests and observation. To be met on my arrival by Claire's reassuring smile put my mind at rest somewhat, and after spending some time with her, returned home once more with a view to return to the hospital again the next day during visiting hours.

Upon my arrival the next day, my heart skipped a beat when I discovered that her bed on the ward had been cleared. A welcome sense of relief was felt upon finding a nurse, who explained that Claire had been moved to another area of the ward, pointing to a curtained section further down. The emotional rollercoaster took another dip upon seeing Claire surrounded by nurses and paramedics. One of the nurses noticed my presence as Claire and I exchanged smiles, taking me to one side for a chat.

The nurse explained how they believed that her health problems were not caused by a chest infection, but in fact a heart problem, whereby the tricuspid valve was not functioning correctly, in addition to what appeared to be a tear in her aorta, the main blood vessel to and from the heart. They went on to explain that this internal bleeding is a serious issue and that Claire was currently being prepared to be transported to another hospital for immediate surgery.

The trip to the hospital, following the ambulance, was spent mostly in a daze, with the flashing blue lights doing nothing to help my state of worry. Once the ambulance had stopped I remember leaving my car with little more than the thought, "they can tow it!" and hurried to catch up with Claire and the paramedics. They allowed us a few minutes together before directing me to a waiting room for the anticipated eight hours that the operation was expected to take. This night had now been promoted to the worst night of my life.

Some fourteen hours later, a nurse dressed in scrubs entered the waiting room and informed me that the operation had been successful; that she was now in recovery in intensive care and that I could go in and see her now. The nurse went on to indicate that her surgeon would be with me presently to explain further the details of the operation.

Entering the intensive care unit was like walking onto a set for a sci-fi movie, beeps, flashing lights and monitors everywhere. Claire, buried beneath a web of tubes and wires, looked peaceful, with a healthy glow now replacing her previously pale complexion. As I sat there, holding her hand, I remember smiling, with a renewed sense of hope that everything will be ok, we'll get through this hiccup and things will return to normal. It wasn't long before a doctor gained my attention and beckoned for a word. After kissing Claire's forehead, and whispering, "You hang in there girl", I joined her surgeon, now stood a few feet away.

First he explained that they had replaced her heart valve with an artificial one. He further explained how they had repaired several rips in her aorta caused by stretching, and that this stretching is likely the result of a genetic disorder called *Marfan's Syndrome*, a disorder largely effecting connective tissue within the body. This was great, it sounded like they had managed to patch her up with no problems, and for the briefest of moments allowed myself to listen to the inner voice whispering that everything is going to be ok.

This moment was indeed brief; as the surgeon went on to explain that they had turned the sedation off some hours ago, and that they would have expected Claire to wake up by now. The fact she had failed to do so meant that Claire was now in a coma. It was suggested that I prepare myself for the possibility that Claire may never wake up. This was not a point I was prepared to concede and dismissed the very notion, choosing to believe that she simply needed a rest and would wake very soon.

On the fourth day of sitting and holding Claire's hand, only leaving her side for toilet breaks and to update the family, the nurses arranged a place for me to stay, only a stone throw from the hospital. Whilst I had no intention of leaving my lover's side until she opened her eyes, a shower couldn't hurt!

Day seven brought with it a blow to my hope, as they began filtering her blood to support her renal functions. I remember whispering something along the lines, "You need to stop this and wake up now", into her ear. The hand holding vigil continues, with by now, a fair knowledge of the function of every machine and wire now attached to Claire.

On day ten, exhausted and in desperate need of a shave, I returned to Claire's side after indulging in my new diet, consisting mainly of coffee. On this occasion I sat on the bed beside her, careful not to disturb any tubes or wires, and said, "Hello sweetheart, I'm back". Talking to Claire this way was not uncommon after being told that although opinion was divided, it may well be possible for those in a coma to hear some of what is said to them. I found myself completely comfortable with this concept in addition to my own thoughts that my familiar voice could help serve as a beacon of sorts, to help Claire find her way back to me. What I didn't expect was for her eyes to move. Now wondering if after ten days of hoping that I had imagined this I spoke again, "Hello darling, can you hear me?" Again her eyes moved, and with a muffled shriek of joy, I hurried off to find a nurse.

Within an hour of first moving her eyes, Claire was responding to questions as best she could without speaking, and breathing for herself. The ten days of coma had taken a toll on her body, leaving her extremely weak, needing water fed to her off a sponge as she was unable to hold anything for herself. We were told to expect an extended stay in hospital, but it didn't matter, Claire had come back to us, we would cope with that trivial detail.

The speed of Claire's recovery not only astounded me, but also the professionals involved in her care. Within a short few months, and after begging the doctors to allow her to come home, even if only for the holidays, it was agreed that Claire be discharged. This took some getting used to, not because I had grown accustomed to her absence or anything like that, but because Claire now ticked like a clock. The artificial valve in her heart could be heard quite loudly whilst in bed, serving as both a reassuring sound, and a distraction when trying to get some sleep.

Within four weeks of returning home, Claire had returned to work, leaving me stunned at the overall speed of her recovery, and impressed with how little she had allowed these experiences to affect her. Claire's trademark smile was once again everywhere I looked, and family life, for the best part, had returned to normal. Three months after her initial discharge from hospital we attended a clinic appointment, and after a series of tests it was pronounced that everything was looking good, and that another appointment would not be required for a further six months.

Shortly after arriving home from a romantic break in Amsterdam that Claire had arranged in honor of my birthday, we made our way back to the hospital for her latest clinic appointment. We were both in good spirits, with a positive outlook, as we sat waiting for her name to be called with the results of the tests undertaken earlier in the day. The doctor indicated that the artificial valve was functioning as expected and that no further stretching had occurred on her aorta. His expression, now changing to one of a more serious nature, preceded his announcement that they suspect further internal bleeding and that Claire, at some point in the near future, may need a further operation. Finally he stated that he would be in touch after speaking to her surgeon.

As soon as we left the consulting room I could feel Claire's despair at the thought of another operation. Indeed the thought of Claire having to undergo any more suffering than she had already endured made me feel quite nauseous and so suggested we grab a coffee in the hospital café. It seemed the longer this new thought had to take hold, the more down and frustrated Claire would get, and so I spent most o this time trying to convince Claire that everything would be ok, and that compared to the previous operation, would be a cake walk. After finishing her hot chocolate, Claire conceded that I was probably right, and the usual smile I had grown to love, returned once more to her face.

As we approached the exit to the hospital, Claire turned to me, the smile now replaced with a look of dread as she dropped to her knees, clutching at her back. I helped her to a nearby seat and then wasted no time acquiring a wheelchair in order to push her round to the accident and emergency department at the other side of the hospital. After explaining the situation, and insisting that they obtain Claire's notes from the clinic she had attended that day, she was admitted again and moved immediately to a ward. A further operation was scheduled for the next day. We were told that unless Claire undertook this operation she would be dead within three days due to internal bleeding caused by another rupture in her aorta. Upon Claire signing the consent forms we were further advised that her chances of survival were only forty percent and that the chances of her having full use of her legs again would be a further forty percent.

The fight seemed to flow out of Claire rapidly, and she was clearly scared. For the next twenty four hours I would not acknowledge these pessimistic odds, instead I would focus upon her amazing previous recovery, and set about convincing Claire that she was an odd breaker. I needed her to fight. She was young, she was strong, and she could beat this as she had done before.

Again, the overwhelming sense of relief was overpowering as the nurse explained that my wait was over and that Claire was back in intensive care. This time, the ten hour wait had seemed far longer than the fourteen from the previous occasion. Once back by her side I was approached once again by her surgeon who explained that during the operation it had been decided that rather than simply patching up her aorta with more grafts, that they would instead replace her entire descending aorta with an artificial one. He also explained that due to Claire's previous coma it would be likely for this situation to repeat itself. Armed with the facts from the previous occasion I immediately inquired as to when the sedation had been turned off, and when she was expected to wake up. Claire's surgeon indicated that a response should be forthcoming quite soon after the sedation had ceased, and so this could be any time.

After about an hour Claire opened her eyes. "Yes, no coma!" I thought to myself as I moved towards her to speak. "Hello baby", I said with a huge grin on my face. After looking at me, somewhat puzzled, Claire replied, "Who are you?" This caught me off guard for a moment, unsure as to whether this was Claire making a joke, or whether she in fact did not recognize me. Before I had a chance to speak further, Claire started to struggle to get out of bed, causing an influx of medical professionals to surround her in an effort to prevent her pulling out anymore tubes or wires. "Yes, she moved her legs!" I thought to myself, as I backed away to allow them space to work.

After managing to get Claire to settle, a doctor approached and advised me that everything was looking good but that Claire was complaining of chest pain when she breathed.

They had decided to sedate Claire once more with a view to putting her back on a ventilator for a while, to give her a rest. I explained the situation to Claire, who seemed to recognize me now, and told her I would be here when she woke up.

After three days of this medically induced coma I was told there were no signs of improvement and that they would keep her on a ventilator for another few days. On the sixth day it was decided that they should wake Claire up, but leave her on the ventilator. This could be achieved with a procedure called a tracheotomy, which would allow her to be conscious whilst still benefiting from the support supplied by a ventilator. The procedure was planned for noon the next day and so I ventured home to update the family and get some rest, planning to return in the morning, before the procedure was due to take place.

Halfway through my journey back to the hospital my mobile phone rang. Glancing at my phone and noticing it was the hospital calling is about all I remember of the early part of the day. Even though I could not answer the phone because I was driving, I knew deep down something was horribly wrong; in fact I was convinced that Claire had passed away.

Everything from this point on is a total blank, up until feeling a hand on my shoulder and a voice saying my name. Upon looking up I noticed that I was sat on the floor outside of the intensive care unit. "Darren, come inside so that we can talk", said the voice, still sounding off in the distance. I glanced at my watch and noticed it was now 3pm and I had lost about four hours. Still in a daze I followed the nurse into the intensive care unit and into a small office where I was invited to sit down.

I was told that Claire had suffered a major bleed on her brain earlier in the morning, and although they had administered treatments to stop the bleed, about half of her brain will have suffered severe damage, and was so bad that she would not recover, she was brain dead, and now only the machines were keeping her alive. I was also informed that the law requires that they wait 24 hours and then conduct a range of tests to confirm brain death, before switching off the machines.

These 24 hours were spent holding her hand, stroking her hair, and talking to her, knowing these would be my last words. The nursing staff obtained a tape player and I played a mix tape containing love songs that Claire had made for me some months earlier, again and again, for the entire time remaining. When the time came, I said goodbye, and held her hand as the machines were switched off, her breathing stopped, and she slipped peacefully away. These last few moments would become etched in my mind, becoming the subject of my nightmares for months to come. An unwelcome action replay if you will.

Upon returning home, in a total state of shock, I had to find the words to tell our three year old daughter that mummy was not coming home. The look on her sweet face as the words sank in is another unpleasant memory that would haunt my waking and sleeping hours. Truly the worst task I have had to perform in my entire life.

Emily and Oliver, Claire's children from another marriage, who had lived with us as part of a family from an early age, were staying with their father during this period. Four days after Claire passed away, and only a day before they were due to return home, their father called me. At first I thought I was subject to some sick cruel joke while he explained that Oliver had just suffered a major heart attack, and had been declared dead upon arrival at hospital. It was suspected that he had suffered from the same genetic disorder that had taken his mother. First Claire, and now my healthy and active step son, aged only nine years old, had been taken from us, obliterating our family within the space of a week, leaving only total devastation in its wake.

And so began my eight year journey through the five stages of grief (as defined in the book '*On death and dying*' by Kübler-Ross), documented in the pages that follow, using a combination of self observations and poetry to describe the emotional rollercoaster, and upheaval, that each of these individual stages brought about for me personally.

Whilst I do not consider myself a contender for poet laureate, poetry seemed the ideal medium to help describe, sometimes quite short lived, yet always powerful, raw emotions. These poems do not always conform to a strict poetry style; however they do describe my innermost thoughts and feelings during times of great personal darkness, and therefore contain a small slice of my soul.

Denial

***Denial** — as the reality of loss is hard to face, one of the first reactions to follow the loss is Denial. What this means is that the person is trying to shut out the reality or magnitude of their situation, and begin to develop a false, preferable reality.* (Wikipedia)

Always a man driven by logic, resulting in an obvious career in software development, my view of the world has always been very black and white, with very few grey areas. The same views extend in to the arena of truth. For me, there is simply the truth, or untruth, therefore my experiences of denial as part of my five stages of grief were relatively short lived.

Having lost the love of my life, and then my step son, whom I had brought up as my own since the age of two, all within the space of four days, my experience of denial was largely encapsulated by sheer debilitating shock.

The passing of my partner had placed me into a state of stupor, whereby I would try not to think about things too much, in an effort to prevent being overwhelmed, allowing the thoughts in at a rate I could cope with. The news of my son's death turned off the thought tap completely, leaving me totally numb and unable to think at all.

The best analogy would be the loud high pitched tone before deafness, or the bright white light before blindness. The loss of my partner produced the bright light, causing me to squint from my thoughts as you would cover your eyes at the sun. My son's death was blinding and darkness created an empty void of my mind.

I think to some extent some aspects of this denial were helpful in as much as they allowed me to get through the two most difficult days of my life, namely the horrendous task of telling our youngest child, at the time only 3 years of age, that mummy would not be coming home. I will never forget the look on her face. When delivering the tragic news about her brother four days later, I found myself with a lot to explain, and managed to do so without thinking about it much myself. I could hear myself saying the words, but it all seemed abstract and off in the distance.

After several weeks, fully aware of the fact I was refusing to allow myself to think, I allowed some thoughts to drift in. Try to imagine if you will, opening the outside hatch on a submerged submarine. You can't just let a little water in through the hatch, and my thoughts were the same, crashing in at a rate where I simply could not keep up with the questions let alone produce any answers. What of our life now? How will these changes affect our lives? How will we cope financially and emotionally? The questions just kept coming.

Reeling from the sheer enormity of it all, I shut it down for a few more days, relying on sleep, and making a constant effort not to think whilst awake. My way out of this conundrum was to take a single question that I had remembered from the onslaught, and attempt to process it on its own. Still no easy task at first, as often an unrefined question leads to many more questions, but this new found level of processing my thoughts allowed me to move slowly through them at a rate that was not so utterly overwhelming.

Most of my denial revolved around a simple thought, "I cannot believe this has all happened, and therefore, I won't." Shutting out my thoughts regarding my grief and loss seemed a necessary defense mechanism that allowed me to take on board these tragic events, in a more reasoned fashion, absent the emotional overload.

There are more subtle ways in which denial following loss can effect a person, sometimes when you least expect it. For myself this operated on both a conscious and subconscious level, with the more conscious refusal to think about the reality of the situation, combined with a more subconscious denial whereby I would expect to see Claire and Oliver at certain times of day, set a place at the table at meals times, or even calling out to them and expecting a reply.

Losing a loved one can be a horrendous and overwhelming shock; in fact it can often be a number of shocks combined. For me, life changing aspects of these shocks were numerous, with the initial tragic deaths, compounded by new found single parenthood, financial implications and the complication of my step children and where they would live. Most people around me at the time failed to see these additional strains on my life, concentrating support wholly on my grief, but these additional worries were mine nonetheless, and all simply too much to process.

I have covered some of the subtleties of denial that I have personally experienced in the following poems.

Why You, Not Me?

You're bright, outgoing and playful,
I'm quiet, introverted and shy.
A sixth sense for what makes me happy,
While the best I can do is just try.

You're caring, selfless and giving,
I'm selfish, and look out for myself,
An Angel on earth, that's what you are,
Plucked from the very top shelf.

You live a healthy lifestyle,
Eat fresh vegetables every-day,
My idea of good health, Is grab a beer off the shelf,
And watch my favorite football team play.

You're love of life was inspiring,
Now I struggle to get out of bed,
There's been a mistake, this can't be right,
You sure it's not me who's supposed to be dead?

You're wandering the heavens above now,
While my pain longs to just be set free,
So I cannot help but ask myself,
Why you then, and not me?

Dreaming Of You

Whenever I close my eyes,
You are always there,
Your sexy smile, your joyful laugh,
Your beautiful brown hair.

When I wake up in the morning,
Wash the sleep out of my eyes,
There you are, with me again,
Not really a big surprise.

As the day passes by slowly,
And all the clocks tick on,
I see your face in strangers,
Hear your voice in every song.

When i get home tired and weary,
Coped without you another day,
I close my eyes and dream of you,
It's not like I have a say.

It does seem quite obsessive,
To cling to your love this way,
I wish these dreams would last forever,
I'd move in, unpack and stay.

A Cruel Stunt

Four days since the love of my life left me,
The memory is still such a blur,
Still scratching my head and asking,
Did this nightmare really occur?

Kick a man while he's down is not sporting,
While lost in the void without you.
The tragedy just keeps on mounting,
How can our son have been taken too?

It's a mercy you weren't here to see it,
It would have ended your fight for sure.
This has to be a cruel stunt that's televised,
Will a presenter be knocking my door?

Goodbye My Love Part 1

They tell me that you are gone now,
Only machines that keep you alive,
But I remember how you came back from a coma,
How you fought with your all to survive.

They assure me there's really no chances,
That they have done all that they can do,
Hold your hand for the next twenty four hours,
And prepare my final goodbye for you.

The seconds they turned into minutes,
And the minutes turned into a day.
My time with you had come to an end,
As you peacefully, passed away.

I can't believe what just happened,
Am I stuck in a terrible dream?
A prayer answered would be to wake up now,
To a comforting nightmarish scream.

Shopping For You

The season to be merry,
Carol singers lurk outside,
Time to hit the shops again,
For the battle of yuletide.

Lost in a sea of people,
Something jumps out from the shelf,
Your favorite beauty brands,
All for pampering yourself.

A box of scented candles,
Some gloves to cover your hands.
Music tracks for in your car,
From the very latest bands.

The ideas keep on flowing,
Never stuck for what to buy.
Part of me, my second skin,
The truth soon forces a sigh.

My basket was still empty,
As I can't deny what's true.
Even though some time has past,
I am still shopping for you!

The Longing

Longing for your touch,
The way you make my blood surge.
Only your caress,
Is needed to stem this urge,

Yearning for your kiss,
A thirst for our lips embrace.
Hankering desire,
For the way you'd stroke my face.

Hunger for your breath,
Body burning next to mine.
Need to scratch the itch,
Feel those shivers down my spine.

Pining for your love,
Craving our hearts beat as one.
Lust, need, want, and hope,
You left, and now there is none.

Our Movie

Longing for a time gone by,
Sweet dreams of days from our past.
A trip down memory lane,
A film, with us as the cast.

Two starring roles, you and I,
Love makes the plot write itself.
Twists and turns with every scene,
Critics would toast our good health.

Story starts with two lovers,
First words spoken were a kiss.
Longing, full of desire,
Feelings we just can't dismiss.

Cut to the montage of love,
Time spent waking hand in hand.
Swear I've never felt this way,
God, strike me down where I stand.

Family life soon takes over,
A baby arrives on the set.
Mother's eyes, bundle of joy,
A smile you could not forget.

The script now needs a rewrite,
The star on your door now gone.
Just the spotlight in my heart,
To light where your presence shone.

Bearer of Bad News

Dolls and teddy bear picnics,
With my girl upon my knee.
Not a manly thing to do,
But this does not bother me.

The room glows with her smile,
So joyous, cheerful and gay.
Yet I'm supposed to tell her,
That mum won’t be home today.

Thinking about the damage,
The sorrow left in its wake.
Putting off this fateful news,
In case there's been a mistake.

"Mummy now lives in heaven",
The smile now falls from her face.
"With us everywhere we go",
"But now in a better place."

Anger

Anger *— "Why me?", "It's not fair!"; "How can this happen to me?"; '"Who is to blame?". Once in the second stage, the individual recognizes that denial cannot continue. Because of anger, the person is very difficult to care for due to misplaced feelings of rage and envy. Anger can manifest itself in different ways. People can be angry with themselves, or with others, and especially those who are close to them. It is important to remain detached and nonjudgmental when dealing with a person experiencing anger from grief.* (Wikipedia)

For the best part, the anger stage of grief came to me as the third stage, after denial and bargaining had abated. This is probably driven more by the type of person you are at your core. Anger is rarely my first reaction to many situations and so it does not surprise me that this stage of grief took some time to rear its ugly head, and it was indeed ugly.

Let's start at the top of the ladder, with the higher power I had attempted to bargain with. Anger usually exhibited itself in this instance with a bunch of rhetorical questions. I questioned the very existence of such a higher power if they could allow such a thing to happen to two such loving and undeserving people. If you do exist, are you good? Are you merciful? Did I wrong you? This list goes on, some just thoughts, other shouted out loud in the fashion of the old cliché, shouting up towards the heavens. All of these questions were accompanied by intense rage. This was not a conversation I was having with myself, but a blazing argument. Being more spiritual than religious, allowed this anger to pass in a comparably short amount of time.

Bringing it back to the reality somewhat, the next target of my rage were the people that had failed to save these two people that meant so much to me. People I had previously held in the highest esteem, those dedicated doctors and nurses that had previously looked after Claire so well, were now to blame.

Why didn't they do more to save them? Why wasn't the cerebral hemorrhage detected early enough to save her? Did the ambulance crew try hard enough to revive my Son? Desperate for someone to blame, these amazing professionals were an easy target. As with my fury towards a un-listening higher power, this misplaced anger was quite short lived after logic prevailed.

The next direction, and not so short lived, was the outrage towards myself, for a multitude of reasons, ranging from blaming myself for being unable to save them both, through to irritation at my own thoughts towards the medical staff. This self loathing soon took me down a path of guilt, replaying every argument, or bad word, ever uttered to either of them, regretting ever having been human with feelings!

Eventually logic took my hand with the fact that people argue, parents tell children off, and sometimes we say and do things we don't mean. Indeed many of the matters I found cause to chastise myself over were not matters of any consequence to them in life, it was me making something of them in death.

Family was next to join the hit list. I think we spend some time convincing ourselves that certain people, when the chips are down, will be there to help and support us. Unfortunately this is not always the case and the stark reality in some cases the complete opposite.

Resentment soon set in when it became apparent that no such support would be forthcoming, and that i would be left on my own to care for a small child. Whilst I have always been very independent and able to cope with life's little obstacles, the principle cause of my vexation was not so much that they were not there for me, but more the fact they were not there for my youngest child, who could have probably benefited from some time away from the a man that is constantly holding back tears.

In hindsight, I accept that I wasn't the best company; in fact I would describe myself for a time as a wandering dark cloud of gloom. These days my anger has reduced to simple disappointment, while at the same time acknowledging that not everyone knows what to say to a person suffering from intense grief, and this can cause many to step away, for no other reason other than their own personal comfort. My family, just like myself, is only human. Grief is a very personal and unique emotional journey, and as such feel there would have been little anyone could have done to ease my feelings of isolation. I felt misunderstood by those around me but nobody could truly understand my own personal experience, as much as I may have wanted them to.

After running out of what I believed to be legitimate targets, anger, being quite some force to be reckoned with, would manifest itself without any good reason, and usually with little warning. My trusty logic served no help here; there is no reasoning with this type of deep routed blind anger.

A good example of these unwarranted outbursts was the deliberate smashing of a coffee cup. I had already dropped one, breaking it in the process. My response, in a moment of rage, was smash another cup! These episodes decreased in frequency as time moved on, more so when I started to actively embrace this rage, in an effort to direct it in a healthier manner, and subsequently prevent the household from running low on cups.

So how did I deal with this frustration? I took several pillow cases and placed one inside the other. I then placed several plastic shopping bags inside the pillow cases and filled those with old glass jars and bottles. On a bad day, where I could feel that it would not take much to push me over the edge, I would take my little sack to the woods, away from people that might point and shout, "Look! A crazy person!", and smash it several times against a tree.

I really can't say just what it is about the sound of breaking glass, but it is most satisfying. After several swings (while wearing eye protection of course), the feelings of rage would be replaced by a feeling of satisfied release, allowing me to go about my day, without haunting thoughts regarding what will happen should I lose the plot, a fear that in itself would be kindle to my anger tinderbox.

My previous experiences of anger within my life had always seemed quite justified, and dare I say rational, whereas the same feeling during periods of grief seemed to have had an irrational element attached whereby I was able to blame anyone, and everyone, for anything. The depression stage of grief followed some weeks later, at first some angry days would be sad days, until the anger had been almost totally replaced by gloom, despair and unhappiness. My poems about Anger aim to depict this, often groundless, frustration with the world.

A Broken Promise of Love

I thought we had an understanding,
I thought we had a deal,
I thought we had a pinkie promise,
But that was not for real.

I thought we had an arrangement,
I thought our contract was sound,
I thought we had an unbeatable team,
No half measures were allowed.

I thought our pact was solid,
I thought our handshake was just fine,
I thought our commitment would last forever,
Survive all obstacles, including time.

If a lawyer for the heart exists,
I should get them on the phone,
Treaty signed and covenants pledged,
A promise broken, you left me alone!

Senseless

There is just a void,
Where your presence were once there,
Empty without you,
And nobody seems to care.

Silent as the lamb,
It has all gone quiet here,
No sound worthy now,
In the absence of your cheer.

Darkness all around,
Nothing worthy of the light,
Everything pales to your glow,
After losing your good fight.

Nothing smells the same,
With your fragrance not around,
Another sense disabled,
Now useless, along with sound.

And now let's talk touch,
Now nothing quite feels the same,
Missing you in all these ways,
But that's just the grieving game.

Fury and Outrage

Myopic with rage,
Fury locks me in a cage,
Justice is not mine,
Full of outrage as I rhyme,
We were robbed of all our time.

Now I start to smash,
Feel relief with every crash,
Standing at the door,
Broken glass adorns the floor,
Still frustrated, I break more.

Feeling better now,
I begin to ponder how,
Anger comes and goes?
Why this is, nobody knows,
Changing tide, one can suppose.

Maddened once again,
This time I reach for my pen,
Let my feelings flow,
The scene, darker than 'The Crow',
Indignation on full show.

Crying Without Tears

No more tears my love,
Doors are closed at the flood gate.
The river may have run dry,
But my cries still resonate.

Crying without tears,
Is like lightning void the bang,
Empty box, on a shop shelf,
A guitar without the twang.

Could I be broken?
Does my plumbing need some care?
Will i ever cry again?
Shed a tear for my sweet Claire?

No Justice

Where is my justice?
No sign of balancing scales.
Expect your life to be fair,
This system of law just fails.

So what did I do?
To deserve a fate so cruel?
Bad in a previous life?
Broke a universal rule?

No jury of peers,
To help keep things by the book.
They would see mitigation,
And then let me off the hook.

This grand court of life,
There is no justice there.
Guilty of a trumped up charge,
The sentence is my despair.

How Dare You

How dare you leave me alone?
To face each and every day.
This is not what we had planned,
Things should not have gone this way.

How dare you treat us this way?
Break our plans for tomorrow.
Smothered all our hopes and dreams,
Replaced with tears and sorrow.

How dare you leave us to cope?
No mother to make it right.
A little girl needs her mum,
Instead you gave up the fight.

How dare you leave such a mess?
Up and leave without a trace.
Your departure premature,
Into Heaven's sweet embrace.

So Angry

Cross that the sun's still shining,
Vexed that the worlds done me wrong,
All day ranting and raving,
Angry, that I must stay strong.

Fury an understatement,
Rage that the world is not fair,
All attempts to console me,
Met with a furious glare.

Hostile to all around me,
My temper soon to be lost,
Life now is too hard to bear,
My heart now covered in frost.

Enraged at the injustice,
Judgment passed, with no appeal,
So hot under the collar,
Fate by the spin of a wheel.

So I'm Told

I'm told things will get better,
By those that can not relate.
Say it's time that I move on,
Now that one I really hate.

Tell me that time's a healer,
Soon I'll be rid of this pain.
To put this all behind me,
And should look to live again.

It all seems kind of silly,
The notion just makes me mad.
Why find it so hard to see,
That it's normal to be sad.

My grief is real and valid,
They just don't know what to say.
Realizing that I'm alone,
It's my hurt, my loss, my way!

Bargaining

Bargaining *— "I'll do anything for a few more years."; "I will give my life savings if...". The third stage involves the hope that the individual can somehow undo or avoid a cause of grief. Usually, the negotiation for an extended life is made with a higher power in exchange for a reformed lifestyle. Other times, they will use any thing valuable as a bargaining chip against another human agency to extend or prolong the life they live. Psychologically, the individual is saying, "I understand I will die, but if I could just do something to buy more time..." People facing less serious trauma can bargain or seek to negotiate a compromise. For example, "Can we still be friends?" when facing a break-up. Bargaining rarely provides a sustainable solution, especially if it is a matter of life or death.* (Wikipedia)

Bargaining began for me prior to Claire's death. While holding her hand as she lay on life support I remember the wild deals I attempted to strike with a higher power. Call them prayers, call them wishful thinking, you may find yourself doing it regardless of religious or spiritual beliefs, it's human nature to have hope. My hope at the time was that it had all been a terrible mistake and that turning off the machines would not have the grave impact I had been told to expect.

Some texts on the subject suggest that the five stages of grief follow a particular order, but i do not agree. In my experience, these stages of grief need not follow any particular order; in fact I would often find myself bouncing between two or three over a short space of time. The transition is seamless in most cases, but in my experience the bouncing periods tend to be a prelude to moving into another phase in the main.

My initial denial following Claire's passing began to be challenged by bouts of bargaining. There almost seemed a sense of urgency to it, as if time was critical, and that if I were to strike some kind of deal to have my love back in my arms, it needed to be done sooner rather than later. It felt as though the clock was ticking, and I only had until they moved her elsewhere to finalize the deal. There was not much I was unwilling to offer at the time. Haunted by thoughts that the wrong person had been taken, my very life was converted into currency, ready to change places in the blink of an eye. Our family needed their mother, especially our youngest. The very glue that held our family together, and shoes I somehow now needed to fill. Trade places with me to make life better for them, was a thought I had some trouble shaking off.

Once the realization had set in, that I could not have things back the way they were, I found myself lowering my expectations, again as a negotiating tactic. Moving on from having Claire back in my arms, I sought other ways to spend more time with her. During these times, sleep was very attractive, as we could spend time together in my dreams. I would spend a lot of time talking to her, sometimes out loud, and imaging a response. I even considered enlisting the help of a medium or spiritualist church. This is a good example of how the distinctions between the stages of grief can become blurred, with bargaining and denial both fighting for my attention at the same time.

My eventual movement into the anger stage of grief brought about a clear end to my bargaining and denial stages. My poems about bargaining look to describe some of these emotions, along with anxiety, something that many grief professionals feel is more prevalent in those having lost a loved one, rather than facing their own death, a topic covered further in the *Epilogue* of this book.

If Only

If only we'd learned of this sooner,
Took action as quick as could be,
Questioned the signs laid before us,
Second opinion? No let's have three!

If only we lived another lifestyle,
Went jogging three times a day,
Off to the gym and then swimming,
Would this have kept fate at bay?

If only I had treated you better,
Looked after you passionately,
Took on more responsibility,
Bore more of our load onto me.

If only I had shown my love better,
Never argued or brought you to tears,
Would you have fought harder to stay my side?
Not this nightmare, my pinnacle of fears.

If only time travel existed,
I'd go back, have our time again,
Looping the loop through our favorite days,
No how, no where, just when.

Bargaining With Thin Air

I would give the world right now,
For your return in to my arms,
Buy every bunch of heather,
And more such lucky charms.

Would not take you for granted,
As you won't always be there,
Make the best of every day,
Give you all my time I swear.

I would be a better man,
The improvement you would see,
I would give you anything,
If you'd just return to me.

Pray to a god in heaven,
Though I never have believed,
False promises I cannot keep,
For this pain to be relieved.

One Priceless Second

Our own perfect place,
Not a care here in the world,
No loss, pain or suffering,
A utopia unfurled.

Our own secret place,
For just one second a day.
A place we can be alone,
And it's not so far away.

Nearly there again,
Before consciousness sets fast,
For a second, waking up,
I forget that you have passed.

I Would

I'd kiss your lips more often,
Make more time to stroke your hair.
Take more pictures of our love,
And the moments that we share.

I'd be a better husband,
Never fail to hold your hand.
Try to see your point of view,
Do my best to understand.

I'd never be too busy,
You would always have my ear.
Hold you tight when you are down,
Help to dry up every tear.

I'd cherish every moment,
Never back down from a dance,
These are all the things I'd do,
If we had a second chance.

Calculation Error

The universe is broken,
There is something not quite right.
Absence clearly present here,
There has been an oversight.

A huge miscalculation,
We're a sum more than ours parts.
Error in the master plan,
To break up these loving hearts.

Is something wrong with Karma?
Was told you reap what you sow.
She was selfless to the end,
So some just deserts should flow.

No more equilibrium,
The balance is off by far,
To take the very best of me,
Left a never healing scar.

Treading Water

Slipping and sliding,
On frozen cold emotion.
Seems to matter not,
The depths of my devotion.
The power of love,
Not enough to bring you back.
All gone off the rails,
Now my engine lacks a track.
Better part of me,
Departed at the station.
Only your return,
Can offer me salvation.
What am I to do?
Facing life alone is grim.
Drowning in a sea,
Treading water while I swim.

The Time Machine

If H.G Wells rang my bell,
With his time machine in tow,
Would I jump, a few years back?
Our first date, be that "no show"?

Avoid all of this heartache,
Feeling like life can't go on?
Walk straight past, the day we met,
Let time now alter the song?

A new time stream location,
Erect an emotion wall?
Set a limit to my love,
To restrict how far I fall?

Go back, and soil our love,
Sabotage everything dear?
Make a premature retreat,
As that fateful day draws near?

Should I use this great power?
To save future loss, and pain.
No, there really is no doubt,
I would choose it ALL again!

Anxiety Attack

I can feel my heart beating,
A machine gun in my chest.
Pretty sure I'm gonna die,
This will be my place of rest.
My breath is short and stifled,
And heart continues to race,
Absolutely certain now,
This will be my resting place.
I'm starting to feel weak now,
And finding it hard to stand.
Prepare now to shut my eyes,
With no-one to hold my hand.
My muscles ache all over,
This chest pain can not be right.
Absolutely has to be,
This day I lose the big fight.
Terror has overwhelmed me,
Void, but for feelings of dread.
There's terror and foreboding,
In this...wait...still thinking head!

Depression

***Depression** — "I'm so sad, why bother with anything?"; "I'm going to die soon so what's the point?"; "I miss my loved one, why go on?" During the fourth stage, the grieving person begins to understand the certainty of death. Much like the existential concept of The Void, the idea of living becomes pointless. Things begin to lose meaning to the griever. Because of this, the individual may become silent, refuse visitors and spend much of the time crying and sullen. This process allows the grieving person to disconnect from things of love and affection, possibly in an attempt to avoid further trauma. Depression could be referred to as the dress rehearsal for the 'aftermath'. It is a kind of acceptance with emotional attachment. It is natural to feel sadness, regret, fear, and uncertainty when going through this stage. The feeling these emotions show that the person has begun to accept the situation. Often times, this is the ideal path to take, to find closure and make their ways to the fifth step, Acceptance.* (Wikipedia)

When a person is Angry, their behavior is usually quite apparent. Depression, on the other hand, can go unnoticed to both sufferers and observers for some time. In my own case this situation was compounded by the very nature of the beast. Being a proud man, I was reluctant to allow anyone to become aware of my current 'weakness', driving my intense sadness and woe behind closed doors.

This particular stage of grief crept up on me quite slowly, at first interlaced with anger and occasionally, denial. Once these other feelings had diminished, the decline into darkness was rapid, and the depths seemed without an end, with each passing day sinking further and further into a pit of my own darkness and despair.

My awareness of my situation began with waking thoughts such as, "Oh great, another day of pain." After a couple of years these thoughts had been replaced by a far more grave belief that my own death would be a mercy. At this point I decided it was time to seek some help from our family doctor.

After explaining my dire thoughts, my new found talent for ignoring my door knocking or the phone ringing, my lack of energy or enthusiasm, and the fact the only thing I looked forward to was sleep, my doctor decided to prescribe a course of anti-depressants. At this point, with the feeling I had nothing to lose, started popping the pills.

In my opinion, whilst this type of medication served well to take the edge of such dark depression, they did not serve my long term needs. Although I do not recommend that depression sufferers avoid seeking medical attention, I would caution against the belief that such treatments go any way towards a cure. My journey through the five stages of grief, the real long term "cure", ceased immediately with the commencement of this medication, locking me into a state of zombie-like apathy. This type of treatment seemed to create an equal playing field for all emotions, both good and bad.

After a year, and realizing that positive emotions such as enjoying a sunset, or the thrill of a ride at the fair, would probably be essential for my recovery, I decided to withdraw from this "opt-out" position and continue my path to recovery without this medication, even if this meant welcoming back the darkness.

Depression without a doubt has had the most significant impact on my day to day life, negatively affecting both my work and family life. One example would be missing out on the true joy of the earliest years of my daughter's life. The years that should have been enjoyed were stained and darkened by the weight of my loss, and subsequent emotional state. Harder still, was the need to keep my emotional delicacy well hidden from her, feeling that she had suffered enough losing her mother and brother, without worrying about why daddy is crying every day.

Looking back I can identify numerous signposts dotted along the road of depression, starting with the day the tears dried up. It is a strange sensation, to be crying inside, but devoid of tears. This signaled the start of a slow and gradual decline in the frequency and intensity of such despair.

Also worthy of mention is the first day I was able to talk about my partner, and step son, without becoming overwhelmed with emotion. Previously, any attempt to talk about them, something I was desperate to do, resulted in choking back tears and unable to speak. Each time i would try to utter a word it would be replaced by the type of half-crying, half-talking one would expect from a five year old child who has hurt his knee. One day the words actually made it out of my mouth, and it felt good. It felt like I was finally honoring their memory by talking about them, something I proceeded to do quite often, much to the annoyance of my friends I suspect.

Another significant obstacle to my recovery was the fear that I may also lose our young daughter to the same genetic disorder that had afflicted her mother and brother. Some five years after these tragic incidents took place, and only once genetic screening technology had improved somewhat, my mind was finally put at ease with the news that she was in fact clear. This weighty burden of worry, now removed from my shoulders, allowed me to take a further step forward, counting my blessings for the first time in quite some while.

Looking back, I feel I could have dealt with my dark feelings better by; hiding it from others less, embracing company at those times I was not seeking to be alone, embracing the times I needed to be alone without guilt, eating better, getting more sleep and taking regular walks. Depression is a natural part of the grieving process, and as the clinical definition previously states, a necessary prelude to acceptance.

Regardless of the advice offered to me by those that meant well, such as, "Try not to think about it", "Keep yourself busy", and "Move on", I do feel that my depression was inevitable given the depth of my own personal loss, and any attempts I may have made to turn my back on this state of mind may have hindered my journey to recovery. I was not ill as such; this was not something that needed a cure. I did however need to heal, in my own time, and at my own pace. Under these particular circumstances, depression is the start of acceptance of the situation, even if accompanied by a host of debilitating dark and negative feelings. My sadness was justified, and I was not wrong to feel this way, for however long it takes.

My poems about depression seek to capture some of these dark moments of depression that I have experienced, along with some of the dark thoughts and feelings of hopelessness that I had at the time.

A Castaway

Dark clouds of despair rolling above,
Obscures the peak of mount melancholy.
Surrounded by a rough sea of sadness,
Waves of woe crashing all over me.

Where is this place i have landed?
A castaway in a far off land.
Beaches of gloom and misery,
Great sorrow in each grain of sand.

I really need to escape here,
Build a raft from my dreams and hopes.
Leave unhappiness there on the shoreline,
And break free of these heavy heart ropes.

Depression is no laughing matter,
Dejection is not a great show.
But no blast of darkness can block out the light,
Just one match can make a room glow.

Dark Clouds

Dark clouds above me,
A world of hurt lay below.
Is this my lot now?
Empty life without you here,
Void of love and your caress.

Dark clouds keep rolling,
There's no escape from the rain.
Now drenched to the skin,
Seeping in through every pore.
I need shelter from this storm.

Out seeking the sun,
To bring new light to my day.
Cold, lost and weary,
Need some solace for my heart,
As it's pulling me apart.

Better off Dead

Let me state my case
How I am better off dead.
Let me have my say,
Now please keep an open mind,
Then choose if I'm in error.

Not been gone too long.
My memories are quite fresh.
Sharp and carved in stone.
Vivid in every way,
Your smell, your laugh, your embrace.

When we meet again,
Would I recognize your face?
The tick-tock of time,
Heading towards the cold dark,
Of age and forgetfulness.

My claim is simple.
My memories will soon fade,
Your face will soon blur,
Join you now while my love shines?
Or a life far more obscure?

Scared to Sleep

I find no solace sleeping,
I am not friends with my bed.
In on the conspiracy,
To keep 'that' day in my head.

All my dreams are the same now,
They don't travel very far.
The tragic day you left us,
Back to the stuff of a star.

One memory that haunts me,
As it's on a loop you see,
The moment, you breathed your last,
That's the dark that awaits me.

Now longing for an exit,
Find an escape, from my dreams,
Finally, my prayer answered,
When waking to my own screams.

Endless Thoughts

Dripping with perspiration,
As mind and body awakes,
A restless night spent thinking,
And so, another day breaks.

Thinking cap on each morning,
Appraise in the afternoon,
Evening contemplation,
These thoughts cannot end too soon.

Pondering over breakfast,
At lunch another review.
Reflect while eating dinner,
All of these thoughts are of you.

Sick of mulling it over,
This study will drive me mad.
A skip day would be useful,
A break from being so sad.

System Scan

Running system scan...
Unknown feelings detected!
Emotional overload,
Your mind is now infected.

Suspect feeling one,
Life no longer holds meaning.
Why get out of bed,
When eyes just won't stop streaming.

Suspect feeling two,
The interface is broken.
No one understands,
Result, few words are spoken.

Suspect feeling three,
All energy depleted.
Fail to face the day,
This error must be treated.

System scans complete.
Grief has steered you for a fall.
No need for alarm,
You are human after all.

So Lonely

Here I am alone,
Just one in a million.
Single grain of sand,
Like a pebble on a beach,
Lonely and lost in a crowd.

Where do I belong?
Feeling lost among the stars.
A spark in the sun,
Merely a word in a book,
And a note within a song.

Drop in the ocean,
A blade on a grassy hill.
Lonesome as can be,
Like a star in the nights sky,
Just one leaf upon a tree.

Language Barrier

I could say the words,
But they would not hear me speak.
Longing to be heard,
Speech with no recognition,
How to make them hear my cries.

How to make them see,
The world through my tear filled eyes,
Darkness covers all,
"Look to the future", they say,
Cannot see that they are blind.

They don't understand,
The darkness, the rage, the guilt,
No comprehension,
They just say I should move on,
But the world looks different now.

They can't smell the truth,
I exist here on my own,
Deep isolation,
All alone in my despair,
Lonely in a crowded room.

Broken

Without your mighty keystone,
The bridge of my life will fall.
Each stone crashing to the ground,
Now just remnants on the floor.

Crushed, smashed and fractured,
Ruins of a time now past.
Yesterday an artifact,
As our future did not last.

How to pick up the pieces?
And where do I go from here?
All these questions haunting me,
But the answers are not clear.

Broken, smashed and splintered,
Beyond all reasoned repair.
Little motive to go on,
When I know you won't be there.

Let You Go

I don't want to let you go,
Nothing's further from my mind.
Just throw you out like rubbish?
And they think they're being kind.

I don't want to let you go,
They say it's time to move on.
It seems to make a difference,
That your presence is now gone.

I don't want to let you go,
You have not long left my side.
Won't stop thinking about you,
Nor your pictures will I hide.

I don't want to let you go,
What they ask is just too soon.
Please end the discussion here,
Let's talk again, next blue moon.

Goodbye My Love Part 2

A tug to the hand,
Brings with it welcome relief.
So many people,
Beady eyes are out to play,
When I look they turn away.

Small hand gripping tight,
My tiny pillar of strength.
Here to say goodbye,
Let the tears begin to flow,
For a mum she'll never know.

Must I say goodbye?
I endured the premiere.
Do it all again?
Just to let these people see,
That your loss has broken me.

Poking at my wounds,
They are not a pretty sight.
Still they peer my way,
Waiting for me to perform,
The first tear would bring a storm.

Acceptance

Acceptance — *"It's going to be okay."; "I can't fight it, I may as well prepare for it." In this last stage, individuals begin to come to terms with their mortality or inevitable future, or that of a loved one, or other tragic event. This stage varies according to the person's situation. People dying can enter this stage a long time before the people they leave behind, who must pass through their own individual stages of dealing with the grief. This typically comes with a calm, retrospective view for the individual, and a stable mindset.* (Wikipedia)

Moving into the acceptance stage of grief was a gradual process for me; I certainly didn't wake up one day and think to myself how great it is to accept my losses now. I would describe my first days of acceptance to be those days that depression had given me a day off. As time marches forward these accepting periods grew in frequency as the lead weights of depression slowly fell away. In this regard I would agree with the view that depression is a necessary stepping stone towards acceptance, and that it is, in itself, the same thoughts and memories, but without the intense negative feelings of hopelessness, sadness and woe.

In my particular case, the first five years of my grief were complicated by the intense worry that our youngest child may have inherited the genetic disorder that had taken her mother, and then her brother at the tender age of nine. A myriad of hospital trips and tests, on an ongoing basis, kept this worry in the forefront of my mind. When the day came that conclusive tests were available, the relief to find she was clear was indescribable.

With this worry abated, I found a small path had been cleared in my mind, allowing me to switch onto other matters related to my grief. It wasn't too long before I had decided it was time to start letting go, and finally scatter Claire's ashes.

These ashes had served as a focal point for some aspects of my grief whereby I would often find myself directing the conversations I would have in my mind (and sometimes out loud) towards Claire's ashes, and so felt like this would be a another huge personal loss. Nevertheless, having decided upon a suitable location, I sought permission, and was subsequently refused based on a National Trust policy. The location in question was a small castle with tremendous meaning to us both, having spent much time there together, and as a family, including the day we met. You could say we considered it was 'our' place.

Claire and I had always been a pair of mischievous practical jokers, and therefore I strongly believe she would have approved of my decision to go ahead anyway, permission or not. I could almost imagine her tittering with naughty glee as we made our way up the many steps to the top of the castle keep. My plan was simple, wait for the right time, check the wind direction (an essential step for anyone considering a similar tribute), let her ashes fly into the wind, and then leave, fast! Arriving home I felt a sense of satisfaction, both in laying Claire to rest in a beautiful place, and letting go of what I perceived to be my last physical pseudo attachment to Claire.

This step brought with it a slice of light to add to my gloom pie, a pie that would emerge from the emotional oven around three years later, perfectly cooked, and now resembling a peace pie. Depression slowly gave way to fond memories and appreciation for having had the privilege to share some time within these people's lives. Photo albums that I had previously avoided looking at because of the intense emotions I had experienced when doing so, were now a source of happiness, with each fond memory forcing a smile.

Obviously, I continue to miss Claire and Oliver desperately, it's likely I always will. I think about them often, but no longer shadowed by the darkness of prior tragic events, now balanced out by all the precious good memories we shared, and the joy they both brought into my life. Sometimes the sadness is there, especially on special occasions, but for the best part my thoughts are now balanced, peaceful, and no longer dominated by my loss, now evened out with my gains.

It has been a long and difficult journey towards acceptance, and there were many times that the feeling of hopelessness, and the belief that the pain would never end, had brought me close to giving up. The belief that the pain was all life would have to offer me from now on was overwhelming at times, with no light at the end of the tunnel. I am thankful for having had the responsibilities of caring for our young child, as this removed many of the more drastic options of these particular dark thoughts from the table quite quickly. Even today I am surprised that I have moved from such a belief to the place of peace in which I now reside, and so find it unlikely that anyone could have talked me out of these feelings with the good old time is a healer cliché, but will argue that time is a changer, of all things.

I hadn't dreamed that this level of peace would be possible, convinced that my life from now on would consist of painful memories, regret, and a constant battle to hold back the tears. There is hope. Things change, emotions change, in fact it is fair to say that I have changed. I am most certainly no longer the man I was before these tragedies struck my family. My views in regards to what is important in life, and what is not so important, have become quite solid and redefined, bringing me nicely to my final point.

I personally do not believe that the (five) stages of grief end with acceptance. I think there may be an important sixth step one needs to take once levels of acceptance permit, and that is learning to *live again*, without guilt, and in a clear pursuit of ones own goals and aspirations.

Grief had a tendency to make me push away, or avoid, many good things in my life, avoiding social gatherings and contact with other people. After making an effort to indulge in more positive pastimes; it was soon easy to see the positive effect it had on my overall emotional well-being, as I hope the following poems depict.

Survive or Thrive

Oh I'd be in such trouble,
If you were here and could have your say,
You'd begin with the fact my life's empty,
One big void since you left me that day.

You'd be sad if you knew I was lonely,
Wish I'd be open to love once more,
You would tell me it is no betrayal,
And throw the guilt straight out the door.

You'd be horrified to see my heart breaking,
Insist that i must let your love go,
Tell me to go live my life to the full,
Because you only reap what you sow.

I will try hard not to disappoint you,
With new dreams for which i will strive,
Because the time has come to ask myself,
Simply survive, or thrive?

Always My Boy

You were only a cute two, the year i met you.
Taking you on as my own, well that was my view.
Age three, your good humor was clear to see.
Always a cheery smile, often giggling with glee.
At the age of four you had started to explore,
First day at school you were the first one out the door.
Once you hit five you had really began to thrive,
Always full of energy and very much alive.
By the age of six you had learned a few more tricks,
Building planes and houses with your little Lego bricks.
Seventh year was fun, always on the run,
Cowboys and Indians with your sheriff badge and gun.
In a flash you were eight, unaware of your looming fate.
But you lived with such a passion, a very endearing trait.
Finally at age nine, right here fate drew the line,
Taking you so early, how is this not a crime?

I Dare Not Look

I stare at the outside often,
Daring to peak inside.
Fully aware of what lurks there,
All of the pain that I hide.

It has never been far away from me,
Never been too far to reach.
The exterior wasn't so daunting,
But the interior I just couldn't breach.

Today something feels different,
I don't have the usual fear.
So I pick up our photo album,
And prepare to fight back a tear.

A deep breath as I open the cover,
Expecting my heart now to race.
Contrary to this, the feeling was bliss,
And a smile spread all over my face.

I thought this would prompt painful memories,
Remind me you're now an angel above.
Of all the pain when I lost you,
But now all I'm feeling is love.

No more tears when I wake in the morning,
No more heart breaks day after day.
I will visit these fond memories often,
And enjoy them in a newly found way.

Forgotten Moments

My worst fear was to forget you,
That your memory would fade,
Slowly eroding thoughts of our love,
As leaves falling from a tree,
Diluted by the ticking of time.

Would I recollect our sweet moments?
Recall the precious love we shared,
Could I call to mind your sweet smile?
Reminisce of your gentle touch,
With a jaunt down memory lane.

Fear unfounded as I finally arrive,
At a new destination of peace,
Folded neatly for the journey,
All our sweet memories packed,
Now with me always as I travel alone.

Always

If there is a life after this one,
I know where you'll be,
At home up there in heaven,
Sat right on god's knee.

Because you were an angel,
Pure of spirit and light,
Looking our for others,
And choosing the good fight.

So loving by your nature,
You would not find a better friend,
Always putting others first,
Right to the bitter end.

I can feel you always around us,
I take comfort in knowing you're there,
And I know for sure deep in my bones,
We'll be reunited again my dear.

See the Sun

I see the sun shine.
No longer through tear stained eyes.
A comforting touch,
The gentle kiss of her rays,
How I have missed this so much.

I hear children play.
The true sound of life reborn.
Music to my ears,
Ringing out to ease my soul,
Pitting hope against my fears.

Breeze upon my face,
A gentle lover's caress.
Wind blows through my hair.
Slipped my mind how good it feels,
When one takes the time to care.

Black Butterfly

I've been gone so long,
There are changes all around.
Life passed quickly by,
With the past now gone to ground.

Mirror on the wall,
Do I even know this face?
Staring back in time,
This me seems so out of place.

Where are all the years?
I was not the man you see.
A self made cocoon,
Now the butterfly is free.

Time to leave my shell,
To stop hiding from the pain.
Take a peek outside,
Learn to love my life again.

Life After Death

Ticks followed by tocks,
The phone rings, and the door knocks.
Hiding from the world,
My cocoon of brick and stone,
Disconnected, and alone.

The warmth of my bed,
Tempts me from the day ahead,
Bull grabbed by the horns,
Look for what I had before,
Seek out laughter, joy and more.

Here I go again,
Yesterday was not so bad,
Had some moments when,
Despite sadness, loss and pain,
I could love my life again.

Life is not so bad,
Now I'm living it once more,
One day at a time,
With each day a brand new start,
You'll be with me, in my heart.

Tenant of my Heart

A huge expanse lay before me,
Where this road leads is unknown.
Thanks to cruel twists of fate,
I must walk this path alone.

Things are not the same without you,
Your absence is still a big deal.
But hope that you're coming back,
Is mere fantasy and not real.

So long I have felt so guilty,
My happiness would be a crime.
But life goes on for the living,
I should join in while I have time.

It does not mean I'll forget you,
You'll always be top of my chart.
And rest assured your place is set,
In the foundations of my heart.

Checking In

Dear love, I'm just checking in,
It has been too long, I know.
Many times I've tried to write,
But the words just failed to flow.

Now that so much time has passed,
And so many things have changed,
Rebuilt from the bottom up,
All our lives now rearranged.

Her hair, no more in bunches,
No more cuddles like a shroud,
Our princess is all grown up,
And would really do you proud.

Blessed with your dazzling smile,
And your beautiful brown eyes,
Also has an awkward streak,
She's your girl, so no surprise.

So I'd just like to thank you,
Hope I have not let you down,
Time to let the flower bloom,
Now our princess wears her crown.

Epilogue

How does my story end? Well, my story has not yet ended. Whilst I may have closed one chapter, my life still goes on, with much of my story yet to be written. The best one can do is share how I feel today, but before doing so I would like to mention some personal observations and issues that I have with the *Kübler-Ross* model of the Five Stages of Grief.

Firstly, this model was originally constructed based on observations of those facing their own death, and then later applied to those that have suffered the loss of a loved one or someone else close to them. Whilst my own experiences have allowed me to relate heavily with four of these stages, bargaining was one aspect I struggled to relate to as strongly as the others.

Curious to know if I was alone in this inability to relate to this particular stage, I conducted a little research. It would seem that many related professionals such as Grief Councilors, agree that perhaps this stage should be replaced with *Anxiety* when related to the loss of another person, and in this respect I am inclined to agree.

Bargaining, when someone has already passed away has a limited scope, they have already gone, and I think this led to anxiety quite quickly once the realization set in that the tragic events had already occurred. My anxiety manifested itself in the first instance as obsessive thoughts about my own mortality, and the lives of others close to me.

Panic or anxiety attacks soon followed, without any particular reason or trigger, just overwhelming feelings of anxiousness and dread from out of the blue. This situation compounded my need to hide away from world, dreading the prospect of suffering such an attack whilst in the presence of others.

My second issue with the five stages of grief model is that in my opinion, there are actually six stages of grief. Whilst acceptance may bring with it the peace one needs to live a productive life, it does nothing to fill the void left by the departed love one. I would like to suggest that *Learn to Live Again* be added as a the stage to follow acceptance, whereby we take positive action in an effort to fill this void with new happy memories and experiences, without guilt, or the feelings of betrayal to the person we have lost.

At the end of my eight year journey to recovery and peace, I found that trying new things once again produced an element of excitement and fun that had been lacking from my life for some time. I started to write, and have previously published several successful non-fiction books of a technical nature.

I would say that this particular book is a solid part of my *sixth stage* of grief and would have been difficult to undertake prior to acceptance, in fact may well have been quite distressing. Today I find myself in a comfortable place, one where I am able to write about my experiences, yes with occasional sadness and regret, but also with great fondness, appreciation and joy. Additionally, I became a dance club DJ and have performed at events alongside some big name artists in the industry, meeting some very interesting people along the way, the whole time feeling Claire's approving presence by my side, and prompting pleasant memories of our little chat room radio station from years gone by.

My desire with regards to this book is to provide some comfort to those that may be experiencing a similar journey of grief. In the first instance I remember how isolated I had felt and how nobody understood what I was going through. I do not consider myself a poet as such, I barely know my ballads from my limericks, but I do hope that my poetry and writings serve to perhaps help the reader feel less alone in these feelings and experiences.

Secondly, my wish is to impart upon the reader a sense of hope, as like me, in time, you will see the sun again. Time is not a healer; however the five stages of grief are a healer, and should not be avoided. Obviously it takes some time to travel through these stages, and exactly how long depends very much upon each person and individual set of circumstances, but most importantly you should make yourself comfortable with your grief, the grieving process, and hang in there.

There is no particular time you should 'move on', or stop talking or thinking about your loss. Your grief is personal to you, and you should be comfortable to grieve, for as long as you need, regardless of other people's opinions or advice. Friends and family will offer advice such as stay busy and keep occupied, however they do not, and cannot, understand the personal nature of your journey, but that too is alright, how could they?

My love for Claire and Oliver is still very real. My journey to peace did not involve sacrificing any part of what these people mean to me. I did not need to forget them, or forget the impact they had on my life. My fears that these sacrifices would be required if I were ever to find any peace were unfounded. The only thing I have let go is the pre-occupation with the pain of my loss, in favor of a more balanced view that included all of the positive aspects related to my loved ones. They did not only die, but also lived, and in doing so, brought great joy to my life. I now choose to celebrate their lives on birthdays or holidays, and no longer recognize the dates they were taken from me.

Is life now a bowl of cherries? No. Life is hard, life is a struggle, but this is no different for anyone. What I can say is that my life is no longer hindered by tragic events of the past, in fact it could even be said that these events have in some way acted as a source of inspiration with regards to how I now live my life. My loss has become a part of me, and no longer all of me. Recovery is not a matter of removing the memory or feelings, but a case of making these things my own, and moving on through my life in a way that my departed loved ones would approve.

My journey through the five stages of grief to a final peace has now ended, and I don't expect anything more than the peace of mind that I have now. But being armed with this new found peace allows me to look to the future once again with some form of hope that a life of happiness still awaits me, whilst at the same time fully aware that happiness does not just drop into ones lap, I must seek it out for myself.

***

If you are struggling, or finding it hard to cope with the loss of a loved one, please see the list of *resources* at the end of this book for some useful links and contact details for help and support. Please also speak to your family doctor who can also offer, or help put you in contact with other local sources of support.

About the Author

Connect

Author's Website

http://www.darrenheart.com

Follow on Twitter

http://twitter.com/darrenheart68

Like on Facebook

http://www.facebook.com/myfivestagesofgrief

Other Books

Other poetry publications by Darren Heart include;

A Suffering Soul, a chapbook containing 20 original dark love poems, featuring poetry that touches upon the darker side of love. Available FREE from most online book stores.

Dedications

This book is dedicated to the following people;

- In loving memory of Claire and Oliver.
- My two beautiful daughters, Millennia and Victoria, who brought light to some very dark days.
- My two very dear friends, Susan R and Juliet C who have kept me sane by offering a listening ear anytime that it was needed over a number of years.
- The doctors and nurses of Southampton General Hospital's Cardio Unit for the impeccable care they provided during Claire's two hospital stays.

Useful Resources

http://helpwithgrief.org

Helpwithgrief.org exists for one purpose - to provide information and support to people who are grieving and those who want to help them.

http://www.helpguide.org/topics/grief.htm

Find expert articles and advice on the grieving process, coping with loss, and what can help.

http://forums.grieving.com/

Grief support groups for coping with loss of a partner, online bereavement forums offering help with grieving the death of a partner, husband, wife or spouse.

Made in the USA
Las Vegas, NV
23 March 2021